HOPE

the story of the blue whale

Richard Sabin
Lorraine Cornish

Published by the Natural History Museum, London

First published by the Natural History Museum,
Cromwell Road, London SW7 5BD.
© The Trustees of the Natural History Museum,
London, 2019.

Some of the text for chapters 1 and 2 used Karolyn
Shindler's articles on Hope for *evolve* magazine as
source material.

ISBN 978 0 565 09477 5

A catalogue record for this book is available
from the British Library.

10 9 8 7 6 5 4 3 2 1

Design by Bobby&Co Book Design, London
Reproduction by Saxon Digital Services, Norfolk
Printing by Toppan Leefung Printing Ltd, China

AUTHORS

Richard Sabin is Principle Curator for Mammals and
Lorraine Cornish is Head of Conservation at the Natural
History Museum, London, and both had a crucial role in
directing Hope's installation project.

CONTENTS

INTRODUCTION

The Natural History Museum is home to more than 80 million specimens that form one of the most important natural history research collections in the world. The Museum's mission is to challenge the way people think about the natural world, and the collection provides valuable reference material to the global scientific community.

The spectacular Hintze Hall (previously known as Central Hall) is the gateway to the Museum's collections and galleries and, in January 2014, the then Director of Science Ian Owens, brought together a team of cross-Museum experts to work on transforming the hall into a natural history museum for the future. Museum staff nominated over 1,000 new specimens for display, specimens that they believed best reflected what is known about the past and deep time (from the origins of our solar system and our planet Earth), specimens that told stories of origins and evolution, and specimens that were relevant to the study of biodiversity and sustainability. After much discussion, it was decided that a new central specimen was needed to link these stories and that the specimen should represent the Museum's hope for the future sustainability of the natural world, and the need for humanity to work together across borders to achieve this. And so, in January 2015, the Museum announced to the world's media that something at its very heart was about to change. The much-loved, iconic *Diplodocus* dinosaur specimen – or Dippy as it was known – was to give up its central position in the Museum's main hall and be replaced.

Very early on, it was decided that *Diplodocus*'s replacement would be suspended from the ceiling, clearing the floor of the hall to help improve visitor access. This meant that the specimen should be an animal – living or extinct – that swam, glided or flew. It had to be a genuine specimen, not a replica, and be able to hold a strong presence in the large space. Attention soon turned to the large skeletons of living whales in the Museum's Life Sciences collection and, specifically, to that of the blue whale. The largest single specimen held by the Natural History Museum is the skeleton of a female North Atlantic blue whale, *Balaenoptera musculus musculus*, which has been in its collection since 1892 and on display in the *Mammals* gallery (previously known as the Whale Hall), since 1934. The two leads on the team, Richard Sabin, Life Sciences Vertebrates Collection Manager, and Lorraine Cornish, Head of Conservation, were asked whether they thought the specimen was in a good enough state of

The blue whale skeleton on display in the *Mammals* gallery, where it hung for more than 80 years.

preservation to be taken down and moved to Hintze Hall, and both agreed it was.

For Lorraine, this represented a literally gargantuan task and one of the biggest conservation challenges she had ever had to face. For Richard, this was a dream come true. As a 10-year-old visiting the Museum he had been fascinated by the skeletons of the large whales – their huge size, their bizarre form and their authenticity, the fact that these were the genuine bones of animals still living in our oceans. Fascinated by animal skeletons, it set Richard on a path of learning and discovery which ultimately brought him to the Museum to work as a curator. Never did he think he would be responsible for the future of the blue whale skeleton that had inspired him as a child.

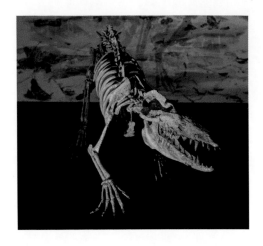

The skeleton cast of the small four-legged land mammal *Pakicetus*, ancestor of all living cetaceans.

FROM THE OCEAN TO THE LAND, AND BACK AGAIN

The female North Atlantic blue whale fulfilled all the criteria needed to reflect the Museum's vision of a natural history museum of the future. The blue whale beautifully addressed the story of its terrestrial origins and adaptation to life back in the ocean. Around 370 million years ago, the first vertebrates emerged from the ocean and began to adapt to life on land. Around 50 million years ago, a wolf-sized mammal living on the coastal margins of what is now Pakistan began the return to the ocean. This was *Pakicetus*, the ancestor of all living cetaceans – whales, dolphins and porpoises. As the largest animal ever known to have lived on Earth and one of approximately 90 species of cetaceans found in marine and freshwater environments across the planet, the blue whale reflects the enormous diversity just within the ocean. And, though its numbers were depleted significantly in the last century through whaling, they have begun to rebound after an international decision to stop hunting blue whales in 1966.

The departure of the *Diplodocus* skeleton cast, which had arrived at the Museum in 1905 and been on display in Hintze Hall between 1979 and January 2017, fascinated both the media and public – many of whom were sad to see the dinosaur being replaced. An ambitious project entitled 'Dippy on Tour' commenced in February 2018 touring the skeleton cast to eight different venues across the UK. The aim of which was to connect the nation with the incredible nature on its doorstep and to celebrate the UK's natural history, and the power of museum collections; and ultimately to inspire the next generation of scientists.

The blue whale skeleton was hung on 8 May 2017 and the spectacularly revived Hintze Hall was officially opened on 13 July 2017 by Patron, Her Royal Highness, The Duchess of Cambridge, with Sir David Attenborough in attendance. This book tells the story of the blue whale, named Hope, from her life to her death to her dazzling re-display, and how recent scientific advances have allowed the Museum to present her in an entirely new light.

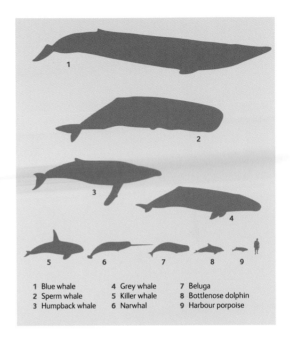

1 Blue whale
2 Sperm whale
3 Humpback whale
4 Grey whale
5 Killer whale
6 Narwhal
7 Beluga
8 Bottlenose dolphin
9 Harbour porpoise

Whales, dolphins and porpoises all have similar shapes but they come in a wide range of sizes from the 30-metre (98½-foot) blue whale to the 1.5-metre (5-foot) harbour porpoise.

CHAPTER 1

THE WEXFORD WHALE

On 25 March 1891, a blue whale swam into the shallow waters leading to Wexford Harbour on the southeast coast of Ireland. Known to be a treacherous area for shipping, with hidden sandbanks submerged just below the surface of the sea, lifeboat pilots were stationed at nearby Rosslare Fort to assist vessels that got into difficulty. On that cold, windswept day, one of the young lifeboat pilots, Edward 'Ned' Wickham, spotted something he'd never seen before – something large and powerful ploughing through the waves.

At that time the people of Wexford had very little experience of whales and of the commercial benefits they could bring. Commercial whaling had intensified in the North Atlantic in the second half of the eighteenth century, but the power and speed of blue whales meant that they would not become targets until the development of cannon-fired explosive harpoons in the 1870s.

Various attempts had also been made to set up Irish whale fisheries in the eighteenth century, but commercial whaling did not become established in Ireland until the early twentieth century and so the people of Wexford were entirely unprepared for the events about to unfold. The whale seen by Ned Wickham ran aground on Swanton Bank, a sand-spit large enough to take the body of the huge animal. Alerting his colleagues at the lifeboat station, they watched as it struggled and thrashed to free itself, but didn't approach the whale for fear of being injured. The next day, the whale had weakened and the pilots were able

to approach it by boat. The animal was beached, lying on its side, and the lifeboat men climbed onto the body. The day before, Wickham had fashioned a homemade harpoon and attached a long-bladed knife to the end. Whether he intended to secure the whale for the money he knew it would bring or just wanted to end its obvious suffering, Wickham placed the blade under the whale's exposed pectoral flipper, piercing its flesh, and then pushed hard down into its body. Local newspaper reports stated that the sea ran red with the blood of the whale, suggesting that he may have pierced the whale's heart, hastening its death and preventing it from slowly suffocating under its own weight. Wickham and his colleagues estimated the whale to be around

Looking towards Raven Point on the north side of Wexford Harbour, Ireland. It was on these shifting sandbanks that the blue whale was fatally stranded.

30 metres (98½ feet) long, but subsequent measurements of the animal showed a head-to-tail length of approximately 25 metres (82 feet).

SALE BY AUCTION

Interest in the beached whale was high and news spread quickly. In 1891, Ireland was governed by the rule of the United Kingdom, and the whale was therefore considered to be the property of the Crown. The law of royal ownership of stranded whales (also called 'Fishes Royal') dates back to 1324 and still applies today around the United Kingdom. In order to raise money for the Treasury, Customs officials declared that the body of the whale was to be sold at auction, and the local Receiver of Wreck was to oversee the sale. The animal had been incorrectly described as a sperm whale, but a local naturalist, seeing the presence of black plates of baleen in the mouth and the bluish-grey colour of the body, confirmed that the animal was in fact a blue whale, *Balaenoptera musculus*.

When the auction was announced, the local community discussed jointly bidding for the whale. In the months leading up to its appearance, fishermen in the region had reported a drop in the quantity of fish being caught and they (wrongly) blamed the whale for the reduction in their catches. Their plan was to

Edward 'Ned' Wickham wearing his lifeboat pilot's gear.

WHALES ON THE IRISH COAST.

Several whales have lattely been reported as having been seen off the Irish coast, and on Saturday the death of one 100ft. long is reported from Wexford. On Thursday, a fisherman named Wickham, being at the entrance to the harbour, saw an unusual disturbance of the sea a short distance out. He plainly discerned the back and tail of an enormous creature who was evidently struggling to get out into deep water. The pilots at the Fort station put out in a boat, but were cautious not to approach too close to the unusual visitor. They continued to watch, and on Friday, its struggles becoming weaker, Wickham ventured to approach the monster, and succeeded in plunging a long knife into the body of the creature under one of the fins. It turned out to be a whale about 100ft. long by 60ft. girth.

open up its belly and recover the lost fish as they did not realise that blue whales feed almost exclusively on shrimp-like krill. The auction finally took place just over two weeks after the whale's death. Bidding was not restricted to Ireland as the press reported interest from a Mr Barnum based in the USA. The commercial gains to be made from the body of the blue whale were potentially huge. Its meat and oil were both worth a great deal, as were the highly-prized plates of baleen, which filter-feeding whale species use to extract their food from the ocean. Baleen – made of a simple form of keratinous protein similar to human hair and nails – had a wide variety of uses in the times before the invention of plastics. Also known as 'whalebone', it was used widely in the production of ladies' whalebone corsetry and other types of body-modifying undergarments.

The auction ended with the whale being purchased by William Armstrong, a local man who also happened to be Chairman of

Measurements being taken by men standing on the body of the beached blue whale.

Many newspapers reported the whale's stranding, describing the commotion the animal had caused in Wexford. The reports included this one, (opposite) published in the *Liverpool Mercury* on 30 March 1891.

the Wexford Harbour Board. Armstrong paid the sum of £111, equivalent to almost £14,000 today. Part of the money raised by the auction went to Ned Wickham and his lifeboat colleagues, who had effectively 'salvaged' the whale and were therefore entitled to benefit. They received £50 (now equivalent to more than £6,000), an amount which no doubt made a significant difference to their lives.

COMING TO THE MUSEUM

When the beached Wexford whale came to the attention of William Henry Flower, Director of the Natural History Museum in South Kensington, London his first thoughts were to acquire it for the Museum. The Natural History Museum in South Kensington

had opened its doors to the public for the first time just under 10 years earlier, on 18 April 1881. Known at the time as the British Museum (Natural History), its creation was mainly due to the efforts of one man, Richard Owen, who had been Superintendent of the British Museum's Natural History Departments since 1856. It was his dream to create a 'Museum of Natural History', with spacious galleries filled with specimens of animals and plants, both living and extinct, from across the world. Amongst these, he envisaged there being a scientific collection of whales and the skeleton of a large whale on display for the purposes of inspiring awe in the visiting public. Owen retired from the Museum in 1884 and so it was left to his successor, William Henry Flower, to try to fulfil that dream. Flower asked Keeper of Zoology, Albert Günther, to enter into negotiations to secure the specimen for the Museum,

A blue whale cruising gracefully at the surface of the ocean.

as the study of Cetology – species of the order Cetacea, or whales, dolphins and porpoises – was poorly represented at the Museum. Scientific staff realised the potential of acquiring such a large specimen and, with Wexford being geographically so close, that the logistical and transportation costs would be far less than for a specimen from further afield. Günther contacted Gerald Edwin Barrett-Hamilton, a young naturalist based in County Wexford, and asked him to find out as much as he could about the whale. Barrett-Hamilton advised Günther to deal directly with the new owner William Armstrong, as enquiries had already been made by other museums interested in acquiring the specimen for their collections.

William Armstrong, Chairman of the Wexford Harbour Board in 1891.

Communications between Günther and Armstrong commenced and, having established that the whale was in fact a blue and not a sperm whale, discussions turned to acquisition not only of the bones of the animal, but also its valuable baleen, which Günther felt would add to the aesthetics of the skeleton when displayed. Little did Günther realise the great scientific value the baleen would have in the twenty-first century, when new analytical techniques would be able to unlock its biological and chemical secrets.

Armstrong's initial selling price for the whale plus its baleen was £250, but he reduced this to £200 when Günther complained that it was too much. Armstrong employed a team of workers to take the carcass of the blue whale apart, and they set about this task with much vigour, though records suggest that they were not used to working with animals of this type. As a result, sections of

the soft-tissue anatomy had already been removed and lost by the time Günther made his requirements clear. The whale had been towed by tug from Swanton Bank to the firmer ground on Raven Point at the end of a long stretch of dunes running along Curracloe Beach. This allowed easier access for the workers and was an attempt to placate the local people and particularly some business owners, who had begun to complain about the smell. Currents carried chunks of rotting whale flesh for a considerable distance along the coast, leading to more complaints as the days and weeks passed. Answers to Günther's specific enquiries about the animal's anatomy led to confirmation that the whale was in fact a female. Günther was particularly concerned that the comparatively small vestigial pelvic bones would be missed by the workers taking the whale apart. Sitting within the soft tissue of the whale on the underside of the body leading to the tail, and completely unconnected to any other part of the skeleton, this

William Armstrong's crude sketch of the beached blue whale with notes on its anatomy.

important evidence of the evolutionary history of whales had become of increasing interest to scientists. It was to be a month before the pelvic bones were finally located and, to Günther's great relief, safely removed.

The final negotiations for the purchase of the whale were made by Edward Gerrard Jr, a skilled taxidermist and articulator who understood the complexities of the skeletons of large animals. Gerrard's father, Edward Gerrard Snr, was a Museum Attendant and trusted assistant of Günther, having set up his own company in 1850 – 'Edward Gerrard and Sons, London'. Gerrard was able to give Günther accurate accounts of progress and ensure that all required parts were collected. Günther had specified to Armstrong that the price the Museum

Albert Günther, Keeper of Zoology 1875–1895.

Telegraph from William Armstrong in Wexford to Albert Günther in London, negotiating the purchase of the blue whale.

Section of the spine of Hope, showing the two, triangular vestigial pelvic bones (bottom right of picture).

would pay for the whale would include 'the skeleton clean and ready for mounting, with baleen'. In May 1891, Gerrard finally used £150 of his own money to buy the skeleton from Armstrong, who really wanted the specimen to go to the Natural History Museum in South Kensington rather than anywhere else. In a summary account to the Trustees of the Museum in February 1892, Günther reported that the final amount paid was a little over £178, which included delivery of both the skeleton of the blue whale and its baleen. Gerrard had ensured that the remains of the whale purchased by the Museum began to leave Wexford in May 1891, bound for London via Bristol. The Museum had secured a specimen considered by Günther to be 'of great importance on account of its intrinsic scientific value and perfect condition.' After the submission of Günther's report in 1892, the Wexford blue whale was given its official registration number: 1892.3.1.1.

CHAPTER 2

EARLY HISTORY OF THE WHALE AT THE MUSEUM

Alfred Waterhouse's original design for the Natural History Museum in South Kensington had included two large wings extending to the east and west along Exhibition Road and Queen's Gate. These were the extra spaces that Richard Owen had wanted to house the existing natural history collections and to allow for their rapid expansion. It was not to be; the faltering economy and problems with the administration of the British Empire led to cuts in Government funding for the project and the removal of the wings from the construction. As a result, space constraints became an issue less than 10 years after the Museum opened.

On arrival at the Museum in 1891, the Wexford blue whale was placed into the vaults for storage as no space was available for it to go on display. Keeper of Zoology, Albert Günther, was overseeing the acquisition of several new, large whale specimens in addition to the blue whale. Whilst some of the larger, older specimens from the Museum's Cetacea collection were displayed in a cramped basement room in the Waterhouse Building, a new – though acknowledged as 'temporary' – structure was built at the back of the Museum in 1895. This corrugated iron shed was

36.5 metres (120 feet) long and 14 metres (46 feet) wide, and had been planned as the place to display the blue whale skeleton. Unfortunately, after preparation of the bones it was realised that the skeleton's length and weight were excessive for the new space and so the bones remained in storage.

The original corrugated iron Whale Room at the Natural History Museum.

The first two decades of the twentieth century saw the study of whales, dolphins and porpoises at the Museum grow, along with its research collection, through the work of Sidney Frederic Harmer, Keeper of Zoology from 1909 to 1921 and Director of the Museum from 1919 to 1927. Harmer established the Museum's UK Stranded Whales Programme in 1913 after negotiations with the Board of Trade and Receiver of Wreck. This led to the systematic recording, collection and examination of animals washed ashore around the British coastline, a project that continues to this day. Further afield, the growth in commercial British whaling activities led Harmer to petition for the creation of a body to monitor what he felt were the damaging and largely unregulated activities of the whalers. This allowed the Museum to send scientists as observers onboard ships and base them at whaling stations, particularly in the South Atlantic, leading to the acquisition of many large specimens. By the mid-1920s, the Cetacea research collection at the Museum was one of the best of its kind in the world. Pressure for storage space continued to grow and, in 1927, the collection of 126 false killer whales from a single mass stranding at the Dornoch Firth on the east coast of Scotland, brought the need for a new display and storage space to the fore. Since the construction of the temporary corrugated iron shed in 1895, there had been periodic attempts to advance

Natural History Museum record card showing the first official report of a stranded cetacean in 1913. Front detail of card (above); reverse card detail (opposite page).

the plan to build a large exhibition hall for the permanent display of marine mammals. The outbreak of war in 1914 had meant the subject was not considered again until Harmer reported to Museum Trustees in the early 1920s that existing displays fell short of accurately representing modern scientific knowledge, and were housed in increasingly unsuitable conditions. Charles Tate Regan, Keeper of Zoology from 1921 to 1927, emphasised the need for the Museum to modernise its facilities to avoid being overtaken by other institutions. The Museum's intentions and critical requirements were communicated to Government in 1923 and by late 1924 plans for a new display hall had been drafted. For the next five years, discussions about estimated costs, lack of funding and criticism of the Museum's existing displays appeared in the national press. In 1927, the Royal Commission on National Museums and Galleries reviewed the conditions in major British institutions. The Natural History Museum in South

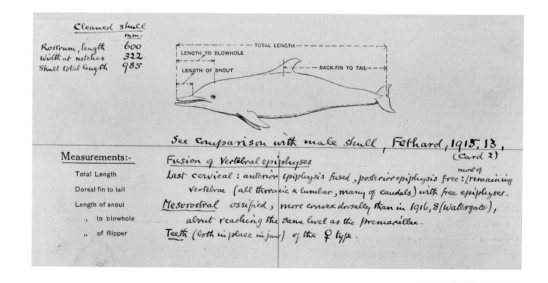

Kensington was highlighted as being in urgent need of expansion. Calculations had already been made of floor loadings and the structural elements required for displaying the wide range of large whale skeletons the Museum now had in its collections. Finally, in 1929, the Government approved plans, released funds and building work commenced on the new Whale Hall (now the *Mammals* gallery).

HOW TO HOUSE A WHALE

The dimensions of the new building were such that, at last, the skeleton of the Wexford blue whale could be considered for public display. Construction of the Whale Hall was completed at the start of 1932. In a special Museum exhibition guide published the same year, William Thomas Calman, Keeper of Zoology from 1927 to 1936, reported that 'The new Whale Gallery was completed at the beginning of this year, but owing to the financial situation it has been necessary to postpone the expensive operation of installing the skeletons and models of whales which it is planned to display in it.' The financial situation in question was the Great Depression, the largest economic crisis suffered by the United Kingdom in the twentieth century. In order to avoid the Whale Hall standing empty, taxidermy specimens of large game animals collected from across the British Empire were relocated from other galleries in the Museum, as were dozens of specimens held in storage. Driven by the efforts of Captain J.G. Dollman, Assistant Keeper of Zoology in the Mammal Section of the Department of Zoology, an exhibition entitled 'Game Animals of the Empire' was to occupy the Whale Hall for the next 18 months.

By late 1933 funds had been made available to allow work to commence on the installation of five large whale skeletons. Finally,

after 42 years in storage in the Museum's Osteological Room, the skeleton of the blue whale was unpacked and taken to the Whale Hall for assembly – the first of the specimens to be installed and taking pride-of-place above all other specimens. The work was overseen by Francis Charles Fraser, Assistant Keeper of Zoology and scientific advisor, and Percy Stammwitz, Chief Preparator in the Department of Zoology. Also part of the team were staff from Edward Gerrard and Sons, London, led by Charles Gerrard. Charles was the grandson of the founder of the company and son of the man dispatched to Wexford in 1891 by Albert Günther to collect the bones of the blue whale. So it was, in November 1933, that a team of men dressed in flat caps, brown overalls and leather aprons began to piece together the skeleton. Working on

The new Whale Hall, shortly after its completion in 1932.

upturned wooden crates on the floor of the completely vacant Whale Hall, the team used planks of wood nailed together to keep the vertebral bones of the whale's spine in position and so allow the insertion of the substantial metal armature on which the skeleton would be mounted. The ribs were attached followed by the shoulder blades and pectoral flippers. Finally, the blue whale's huge skull was wheeled into position and attached to the armature holding the rest of the skeleton. The two enormous bones of the lower jaw were secured to the skull using triangular metal frames bolted through the skull. The spaces between the vertebrae, occupied by discs of fibrocartilage in life, were packed with paper and plaster and painted brown for aesthetic effect. The spaces between the small bones of the pectoral flippers were given the same treatment. In total, 220 bones had been mounted onto the metal armature. Fraser and Stammwitz had kept an eye on the work, ensuring the correct articulation and positioning of the bones. Knowledge of the skeletal anatomy of large whales had advanced in the decades since the blue whale stranded in Wexford, but this was based primarily on beached, often bloated carcasses or those hauled out of the sea by teams of whalers for flensing. As a result, though considered accurate at the time, the positioning of the ribs of the blue whale was significantly incorrect, giving the body of the whale an unnaturally wide appearance.

Assembly of the blue whale's spine and modelling of the cartilaginous discs between the vertebrae. The skull is in position at the far end of the spine.

On 22 February 1934, the weight of the blue whale skeleton was transferred from the floor to the overhead hoisting gear. It remained suspended just above floor-level overnight to allow for any weaknesses and distortion to be checked and for the bones to settle on their armature. The weight of the specimen, complete with armature, had been estimated at 10 tons, and the 5-centimetre (2-inch) diameter steel cables to be used in the final suspension had each been made with a breaking-strain of 15 tons. The next morning, an inspection revealed that all was in order and over the course of the day the skeleton was

The fully assembled skeleton of the blue whale being hoisted into position to allow attachment of the five suspension cables.

hoisted into position to allow the suspension cables to be attached to the five fixing points on the armature. In the absence of anything like today's Health and Safety regulations, men climbed ropes and used dizzyingly tall wooden ladders to scramble across and around the skeleton, steadying it as it was raised. Although the hoisting gear became jammed, leading to a precarious overhead operation to release it, by the end of 23 February the blue whale skeleton was in its final position. After 42 years in storage and three months of preparation, the Natural History Museum now had the largest articulated whale skeleton on display anywhere in the world.

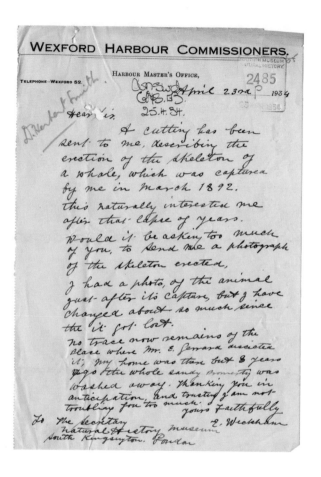

THE TALE OF A MISSING TAIL BONE

When the work was completed and the huge specimen was finally in place, the scaffolding and ladders were taken down, leaving the skeleton hanging majestically in free space. Charles Gerrard surveyed the scene, satisfied with the results and patted the pockets of his brown, workman's overall. He felt the outline of something small in

Letter from Edward 'Ned' Wickham to the Museum upon hearing of the display of the Wexford blue whale. Wickham incorrectly gives the date of 'capture' as 1892.

one of the pockets. Lifting the object out, he saw it was one of the small bones from the spine of the whale. In fact, it was the very last bone in the sequence – actually the fused terminal caudal vertebrae – no bigger than a ping pong ball and weighing less than a chicken's egg. Placing the bone back in his pocket, Charles Gerrard left the scene, taking the bone with him. It would be 82 years before the bone returned to the Natural History Museum.

In January 2015, when the Museum announced that the blue whale would replace the *Diplodocus* cast in Hintze Hall, Richard Sabin confidently stated in media interviews that 'the skeleton is wonderfully complete'. But it emerged that this was not quite true. In October 1987, Martin Sheldrick, Curator of Marine Mammals in the Department of Zoology had received a letter from a Mr Bari M. Logan. The letter was accompanied by the plaster cast of a small bone and details of how the original bone had come into the possession of Mr Logan's family. Sheldrick replied to Mr Logan and informed him that the cast did appear to resemble the last 'caudal vertebra of a mammal and could well be that of a whale'. The letter, along with the cast from Mr Logan disappeared into the Museum's Mammal Section archives until March 2015, when Mr Logan made contact once more. Writing to the Director, Sir Michael Dixon, Mr Logan recounted the story of the bone and his previous contacts with the Museum. The letter was passed by the Director's office to Richard Sabin for comment. Richard had no knowledge of the previous contacts and when he read the account of the bone, was both amused and aghast in equal measure.

Mr Logan's letter recounted the story of Charles Gerrard's involvement in the assembly of the blue whale skeleton in 1933 to 1934 and went on to describe how, as Gerrard stood admiring the work along with invited Museum dignitaries, he put his hand into his right pocket and to his embarrassment, realised it contained a bone from the blue whale. Gerrard apparently said nothing as he felt it would have been too costly and time-consuming to re-erect the scaffolding. As no-one had noticed it missing, he kept the bone and it became a cherished family secret. Mr Logan's family were friends with Charles Gerrard and during one of their visits, he told them the story of the bone, which he referred to as the whale's 'coccyx' (the term for the vestigial tailbone in the human spine). Mr Logan was so enamoured of the story, he told Charles that if he left the bone to him in his will, he would write to the Director and inform him that the blue whale skeleton in the Museum's possession was not complete. Charles Gerrard died in 1971 and some years after this, the bone finally came into Mr Logan's possession. He kept his word and wrote a letter to the Museum's Director, Ronald Henderson Hedley, providing photographs of the bone and a plaster cast to allow comparisons to be made with the skeleton of the blue whale. According to Mr Logan, he did not get much of a positive response but 'more of a guarded reply'. Following up, in 1987 he again wrote to the Museum, this time to Martin Sheldrick, once again telling the story and sending a cast of the bone. This is the letter that languished in the archives until a further 2015 letter to the Director. Finally, it became the responsibility of Richard Sabin. Replying to Mr Logan, Richard stated that upon receipt of the specimen from Ireland, the Museum was not given a detailed inventory listing every bone of the skeleton (221 in total on average for a blue whale, though 51 of these form or relate directly to the skull). If there had been an inventory for the bones of the spine, with each being quantified and numbered pre-articulation, then checked again post-articulation, the

The missing fused terminal caudal vertebrae of the blue whale.

absence of the fused terminal caudal vertebrae would have been noticed. Photographs from the construction phase of the blue whale skeleton showed that the individual vertebrae (certainly the larger ones) were marked in white with a sequential number from the head-end to the tail-end, to aid the men with the assembly. Richard invited Mr Logan to visit the Museum and see the skeleton being prepared for its move to Hintze Hall. His plan was to gently encourage Mr Logan to bring the bone to the Museum for inspection. In June 2016, Mr Logan arrived at Richard's office clutching a small, well-wrapped package containing the errant bone. Examining the bone, Richard agreed that it did indeed look like the fused terminal caudal vertebrae of a large whale. Mr Logan said that he had discussed the matter of the return of the bone with his son Robert, who agreed that the time was right to make the skeleton complete. One week later, Richard was able to send Mr Logan a photograph of the missing bone lying on a table in sequence with others from the blue whale's spine. The bone had been beautifully cared for over the years, now it was back where it belonged and, though small, would finally take its place as an important part of the tail of the whale.

The caudal vertebrae from the end of the blue whale's spine. The final bone on the left is that returned by Mr Bari Logan in June 2016, after an absence of 82 years.

CHAPTER 3

WHALE ON THE MOVE

The first task for the project team was to establish if it was possible to safely suspend the whale from the arches in Hintze Hall without causing any damage to the Grade 1 listed building.

The whale had been suspended from five pairs of cables in the *Mammals* gallery and, in a fortuitous coincidence, the roof of Hintze Hall is supported on five metal arches. To find out the load-bearing capacity of the arches in Hintze Hall, building specialists needed to examine the structure of the arches up-close and take measurements at various intervals. With a height of up to 21 metres (69 feet) above ground, this was not an easy job. Over the course of two nights a small temporary platform was constructed on the main stairs in Hintze Hall and climbers from a high-level access company accessed the bottom of the arches using ropes and determined the thickness of the iron and the Victorian construction methods, enabling a structural engineer to determine the load-bearing capacity of each arch.

To find out the weight of the whale a team climbed into the loft above the *Mammals* gallery into which the specimen's 10 suspension cables ran. The cables were looped over heavy steel beams, two per beam. Each beam was gently jacked up a few millimetres, taking the weight onto a load cell to register how much weight each carried. Knowing exactly how heavy the skeleton was and how the weight was distributed was vital in determining if and how it could be suspended in Hintze Hall. Reports from the 1930s archives put the figure at 10 tons but,

from more recent published weights of similar whales, the true figure was suspected to be much less. And, after some careful calculations plus the addition of some contingency, the final working figure was estimated to be 4.3 tons for the whale skeleton and its steel armature. The team were relieved to discover that this was within the weight-bearing capacity of the ceiling arches in Hintze Hall. Now the Museum needed to seek official permission from English Heritage and the Royal Borough of Kensington and Chelsea. After a detailed consultation, a Listed Building Consent application was submitted and permission was granted.

The next step was to acquire accurate dimensions of the skeleton to help plan its new mount. This was done using a LiDAR

The scaffold is installed around the blue whale under the watchful eye of the animal models in the *Mammals* gallery.

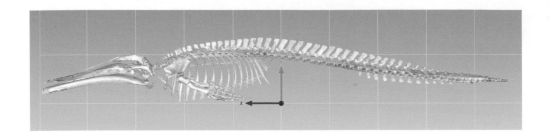

(light detection and ranging) scan while the whale was still suspended in the *Mammals* gallery. A LiDAR scan uses pulsed laser light to measure distance. Pulsed onto the skeleton surface, the difference in laser beam return times and wavelengths was used to make an accurate digital 3D representation of the whale.

LiDAR scan of the blue whale skeleton to create accurate measurements to help in the planning of the new mounts.

FACE TO FACE WITH THE WHALE

Until this phase of the project it was assumed that the condition of the whale skeleton was good enough for it to be disassembled and re-suspended. But the exact condition of the bones and whether they would withstand the strains and stresses of dismantling, transportation and remounting had to be tested. Its position in the *Mammals* gallery presented substantial access challenges – it was suspended directly above a life-size model of a blue whale and surrounded by four other whale skeletons and a zoo of taxidermy specimens beneath, so a scaffold structure was required.

The conservation team needed a minimum of four months to clean the surface of the whale, and to assess and dismantle it. But to close such a popular gallery for this length of time was simply not an option. The compromise was to close for just three weeks to install scaffold, then reopen to the public while the cleaning and dismantling was carried out – allowing visitors to see conservation in action. A specialist scaffolding company was employed to carefully thread the scaffolding poles between the surrounding specimens, and finally in October 2015 the team were able to climb the scaffold for a closer look. The initial inspection was positive and the skeleton, although carpeted in a thick layer of dust, looked to be in relatively good condition.

With a surface area of approximately 110 square metres (1,180 square feet) to clean, the conservation team used soft brushes and portable vacuum cleaners to remove the dust from the bone surface. Approximately 1.3 kilogrammes (3 pounds) of dust was removed in total and later analysed. Apart from being unpleasant to look at, there are other reasons why dust shouldn't be left on specimens. Dust is hygroscopic, meaning it attracts water, which is particularly bad for bone as it can aid the breakdown of collagen – one of bone's main components. Dust can also house and be a source of food for Museum insect pests that have the potential to cause damage to a range of other museum specimens.

Layers of thick dust being removed from the skeleton using a soft brush.

The dust from the whale was examined using different analytical techniques. Samples were taken and mounted onto a glass slide then placed in a confocal microscope, which scanned the dust using a laser beam. The laser excites the natural fluorescence within the dust, revealing the different materials and their chemical differences. Organic and

inorganic materials were found from a variety of sources, including the building itself, various airborne pollutants, skin and particles of clothing.

The dust was also analysed using a process called X-ray diffraction, which shows up any inorganic material. Each tiny mineral particle, present as a crystalline solid, has a unique characteristic X-ray pattern, like a fingerprint, that identifies it. X-rays are passed through a prepared

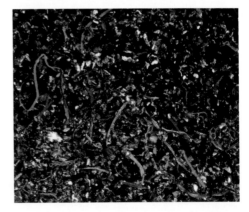

sample and, by measuring the angles and intensities of the diffracted beams, an X-ray pattern is formed that can be compared to a set of reference materials. The following minerals were identified in the dust: calcite, quartz, gypsum, mica, kaolinite, talc and smectitic clay. By collecting information on the quantity and composition of the dust, scientists can find out what the main source of the dust is and if there is any seasonality in its composition and the amount of dust laid down. This information is documented in association with the specimen and its condition and can help the planning of cleaning strategies.

The next phase of work involved recording the condition of the blue whale. Each skeletal element was painstakingly inspected and photographed to document any signs of fragility and weakness. Measurements and samples were taken for analysis and any features of interest were mapped onto diagrams to show areas such as loss of bone, cracking, delamination, staining, leaching lipids, old fillers, metal supports and inserts. The report formed the basis of recording any change in condition as the project progressed. A second more detailed evaluation took place after the whale had been de-installed, and the final detailed report provides a permanent record and baseline for any future work that may be carried out.

Traditionally, specimen preparers and sometimes even conservators

Cleaning dust from inside the rib cage using a portable vacuum cleaner (opposite).

A confocal microscope image of dust from the whale skeleton showing different fibres and particles (opposite bottom).

One of the thoracic vertebrae showing historical cracks and damage around the original mount.

discreetly 'leave their mark' on any significant specimen they have worked on. So it was no surprise when the signatures of the original team that placed the skeleton in the gallery back in 1934 were discovered on the underside of the skull. Richard and Lorraine were particularly pleased to see the signature of Charles Gerrard present. It had been Charles's father Edward Gerrard Jr who had been key to securing the purchase and safe delivery of the blue whale to London.

REMOVING THE SKELETON

The dismantling of the blue whale skeleton from the *Mammals* gallery was a challenge. The skeleton is 25 metres (82 feet) long, weighs over 4 tons and contains more than 220 bones. The skull spans almost 6 metres (20 feet) in length with more than 46 bone elements fused or partly fused together – the jawbones of blue whales are the largest single bones to have ever existed, and each of the blue whale jawbones weighs around 500 kilogrammes (1,100 pounds), roughly the same as an adult male polar bear.

Signatures of the original team who constructed and installed the skeleton back in 1933 and 1934.

The first phase involved careful planning and extensive labelling of each bone and assessing the condition of the metal armature, which ranged from small metal rods, staples and nails to large metal bolts, rods and straps – some of which exhibited slight to severe corrosion. An assessment of the existing armature was completed and a decision was made to remove the armature where possible. It became clear from drill holes and cut marks that the skeleton was originally articulated and mounted in quite a brutal fashion.

The de-installation itself was like trying to work on a large, three-dimensional puzzle. Not all parts of the skeleton could be reached at the outset so careful planning was required. For example, the ribs had to be cleaned and removed before further scaffold could be constructed to provide access to the highest vertebrae of the back. A team of professional object handlers were employed to assist the conservators in the heavy work of dismantling the skeleton, working closely with the conservation team, they advised on how to handle each element to ensure that the bones were removed carefully and without damage.

On 26 October 2015 the team began to dismantle the skeleton, starting with the removal of the smallest caudal vertebrae. The first

Members of the conservation team labelling each part of the skeleton before de-installation.

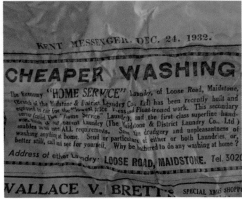

KENT MESSENGER. DEC. 24, 1932.

CHEAPER WASHING

The Economy "HOME SERVICE" Laundry, of Loose Road, Maidstone, (branch of the Maidstone & District Laundry Co., Ltd) has been recently built and equipped to cater for the "lowest price" Press and Float-ironed work. This secondary service (called the "Home Service" Laundry), and the first class superfine handwork done at our parent Laundry (The Maidstone & District Laundry Co., Ltd) enables us to meet ALL requirements. Save the drudgery and unpleasantness of washing anything at home. Send for particulars of either or both Laundries, or, better still, call and see for yourself. Why be bothered to do any washing at home?

Address of either Laundry: LOOSE ROAD, MAIDSTONE. Tel. 3020

WALLACE V. BRETT'S SPECIAL XMAS SHOPP

task was to remove the plaster covering at the very end of the tail section so the initial vertebra could be released. To remove any of the vertebrae, the plaster-modelled intervertebral discs had to be chiselled away so that the central armature was exposed and the vertebrae were loosened from the mount. This was complicated by the fact that underneath the plaster there were a large number of wooden splints and wedges holding each vertebra firmly in place. These were often nailed directly into the bone by the 1930s team, so some reverse engineering was needed to extract each bone from the armature. As each vertebra was removed, the team learned more about how the skeleton was articulated.

When the team reached the cervical vertebrae the task of removing each one became more difficult as they were packed tightly together. However, the added bonus was that the team discovered that a large quantity of newspaper had been used as packing material. The newspaper pieces dated between 1932 and 1934 and have been preserved where possible to add to the archive documentation of this project.

The ribs were each carefully removed by hacksaw – the only way to remove them without damaging the bone.

Scraps of a 1930s newspaper were discovered during the dismantling process.

After the body of the skeleton had been removed, the scaffolding was altered so the team could reach the skull and mandibles. The mandibles were unbolted from the underside of the skull and placed in custom-made wooden frames, before being lowered to the ground. The mandibles proved too large to fit through some internals doorways, so were lifted by crane out of the side of the *Mammals* gallery where they were transported by lorry to a temporary pop-up conservation studio in the Darwin Centre.

The skull was the final piece of the skeleton to move. But the team faced a challenge – how to do so without putting strain on the bone, and how to manoeuvre it between the scaffolding and cables supporting the blue whale model beneath. To do this the 900 kilogramme (2,000 pound) skull had to be rotated 90 degrees using a custom-designed cradle weighing the same, putting the total weight at almost two tons. The cradle had been designed to be placed underneath the skull and existing holes, and bolted areas of the skull were used to attach it to the cradle. The conservators were extra vigilant at this stage, ensuring that sufficient support could be given to the skull to keep it attached to the cradle. An additional support was added to the back of the skull to attach it more securely to the cradle, and plastazote foam was used to protect areas around the rostrum. Crack monitors were placed at existing vulnerable parts of the skull to provide a recording mechanism for any cracks that might open up during the process. Removable sides were then added to the cradle, to provide extra protection for the rotation and subsequent move. It was then squeezed very slowly through the gaps – at times with only centimetres to spare – and lowered to the ground.

Taking a blue whale skeleton apart takes up an awful lot of space, and conservation had to be carried out in three different places. The Museum's Large Vertebrate Store was used to store

and treat some of the vertebrae. A pop-up conservation studio housed in the Darwin Centre was used for the mandibles and the other skeleton elements. And the large 6-metre- (20-foot) long cranium was taken to an offsite store, where there would be enough space to build a small platform for access and to carry out the required conservation treatments.

The team discuss preparations for removing the skull and mandible.

CONSERVATION TREATMENTS AND SCIENTIFIC ANALYSIS

It was easier for the conservation team to inspect each bone for damage and prepare treatment proposals after the whale had been dismantled, and then carry out research into a range of conservation issues including how the specimen had been constructed for display and how it had deteriorated over time. By assessing the conservation challenges, effective conservation treatments can be developed, often leading to the discovery of previously unknown information relating to the specimen itself. Conservation science is vital to the ongoing care and preservation of all museum collections. It involves the study of objects before,

The whale skull rotated onto its side, safely supported in a bespoke steel cradle.

41

during and after conservation treatment, and contributes to a better understanding of specimens and the mechanisms by which they deteriorate. These studies help to determine the best conditions for display and storage of objects to prevent further decay. Unfortunately, little information was documented about the condition of the blue whale skeleton at the time of original preparation and articulation.

The Darwin Centre pop-up conservation studio where the skeleton was treated.

One of the first tasks was to carry out an exterior investigation to identify the materials used or found on the skeleton and determine what was part of the specimen and what were contaminants. It became obvious, after close examination, that the historical repairs were all fabricated using similar techniques, with the same materials and completed around the same time. The old repairs were composed of plaster of Paris, reinforced by metal wires inserted into drilled holes on either side of each repair. Many materials were present on the bone surface including oils, chemicals and paint. As the specimen was originally prepared for display in the nineteenth century, it was important to ensure any chemicals or paint found weren't toxic before attempting to remove them. At that time specimens were often coated in pesticides to protect against pests. Unfortunately, these pesticides contained heavy metals such as arsenic, lead and mercury, which sometimes remain on the specimens. X-ray fluorescence (XRF) was used to help identify any potential hazards. XRF is a common type of analysis used in conservation that provides a breakdown of the different elements that may be present in a material. It works by firing X-rays at a substance or material to excite the atoms within it. These atoms then release energy – fluorescence – and this is captured by a detector. The fluorescence is different for every atom and is analysed to determine what the substance is made of. For example, the brown paint on the bone surface contained a small amount of lead.

Patches of leached oil were found on most of the bone surfaces. When they are alive, whales carry a thick layer of fat or blubber in the soft tissue of their body for food storage and heat insulation, and large oil reserves in their porous bones. Following preparation of a whale skeleton to remove the soft tissue, the bones can retain high oil content – particularly bones with a spongy (porous) structure – so it is quite common for oily patches to develop over time, even in a well-prepared specimen. This oil not only oxidises and becomes unsightly, but the sticky residue attracts dust and can cause bacterial growth on the surface of the bone. The oil can also be acidic, so can potentially damage the bone by weakening its structure. Several samples of oil were taken from the bones and the samples were soaked in a pH-neutral water and then tested using a pH meter. The results indicated that the oil was indeed slightly acidic so removing the surface oils formed part of the treatment plan. Multiple chemical treatments were tested to find which was the most effective for the removal of paint and other surface coatings, and the patches of oil; ethanol was finally selected.

In conservation, one of the most complex questions is how much to clean a specimen. The overall final appearance of the whale skeleton is paramount, but the effectiveness, ethical implications and consequence of the cleaning treatment on any scientific analyses of the bones are equally as important. Cleaning specimens can be carried out in many ways but the two main types are mechanical and chemical. One is essentially a dry clean using mechanical force to break the bond between the dirt and the bone surface; the second involves a wet clean that breaks chemical bonds of whatever contaminant is on the surface. The team's approach was to carry out less invasive dry cleaning for most of the skeleton and then to wet clean with ethanol for the more problematic areas containing paint or oil. The individual bones were cleaned using a soft brush and low-suction vacuum, followed by a sponge made from vulcanised rubber which helped remove more ingrained dirt, dust and debris. After the first clean the team focused on removing oils and small areas of paint. Cotton swabs were used to control the level of cleaning and to reach those parts of the bone that were hard to access.

A large gap in the thoracic vertebra was filled with microballoons to ensure it remained stable and strong over time.

The process was one of 'minimal intervention' – doing as little as possible. Any adhesives or protective coatings applied had to be reversible so that in the future they could be removed if necessary. Some areas of bone were friable and crumbling so an acrylic-based polymer, Paraloid B44 (a type of adhesive), was chosen to help strengthen and stabilise the bone, and withstand the varying temperatures in Hintze Hall. Other adhesives were chosen to ensure that the repairs would remain stable over time.

Another material used for repairing cracks or detaching bone was polyvinyl butyral, Butvar B98 – it is a strong adhesive that ages well and can withstand various changes in the environment. Plaster of Paris was chosen to fill and reconstruct any damaged areas as it also ages well and is sympathetic to the bone and easy to use.

Smaller areas were filled using Paraloid B44 and tiny hollow glass spheres called microballoons.

The huge skull was by far the biggest conservation challenge, involving reducing the excess oil, cleaning, repairing any friable surfaces, adhering bone fragments in place and making new fills for large cracks or gaps. Cleaning, stabilising and conserving such a large and complex object can be time consuming and over 700 conservation hours were spent on this part of the skeleton alone.

Reversible filler was used to repair the vertebra.

Once the filler sets it is painted over with acrylic in a similar colour to the original bone, to make the repair less visible.

REMOVING THE METAL SUPPORTS AND ARMATURE

After the metal elements were removed from the skeleton they had to be replaced and, to avoid further strain on the skeleton, only pre-existing holes were used when the whale was re-mounted. The conservation team planned to replace smaller pieces of armature using carbon fibre, which is extremely strong and stable, leaving the larger pieces to a specialist company, the Canadian company Research Casting International (RCI) to create. This company is best known for producing dinosaur models for the film *Jurassic Park* and joined the team in January 2016 so the armature design could be developed in parallel with the conservation work.

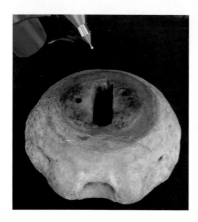 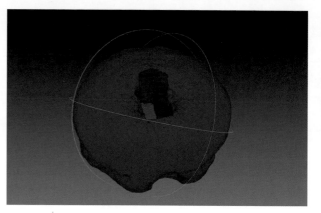

Microcomputed tomography (CT) scanning was carried out on the eight smaller caudal vertebrae at the tail end of the whale – the remaining vertebrae and postcranial bones are too large for the Museum scanner – to produce a 3D image of each bone, so the internal structure could be examined without causing any damage. CT works by illuminating an object with X-rays while it is rotating. The X-rays are collected in a series of several hundred image slices from multiple angles, and the slices are then pieced together to produce a single 3D image. These images not only provide information about possible deterioration in the interior structure of the bone but can also highlight other things not visible to the naked eye, for example, additional metal pieces inserted into the bone and exactly where they were embedded.

Whilst the team were cleaning the left and right pectoral flippers, they noted that the phalanges – 'finger' bones – appeared markedly different from one another. XRF analysis confirmed what was already suspected – some of the phalanges in the right pectoral flipper were not original bone, but realistic plaster reconstructions, and wood and straw had been used in the

Scanning the surface of one of the caudal vertebra using a hand held laser.

Once the vertebra had been surface scanned it could be viewed on a computer as a 3D virtual model that could be studied by others remotely.

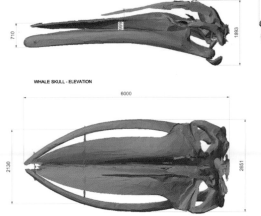

WHALE SKULL - ELEVATION

WHALE SKULL - FROINT

WHALE SKULL - PLAN

reconstruction. Large beached whales often roll onto their right side when they become stranded, so perhaps this caused the bones in the right flipper to become crushed and damaged when the whale died in 1891.

As well as the original LiDAR scan that was taken while the whale was on display, the conservation team captured a scan of each individual skeletal element while the skeleton was being conserved. High-resolution 3D surface scanning of the Museum's blue whale will enable more research to be carried out and data to be collected from the specimen. For example, the detailed scan of the skull and mandibles could contribute towards scientific understanding of the biomechanics involved in the feeding mechanisms of whales, whilst the data from the postcranial skeleton could be used to investigate evolutionary adaptations to life in the ocean. The Museum's specimen is a North Atlantic blue whale, *Balaenoptera musculus musculus*, but other subspecies occur across the world's oceans. Data from scanning can be used in conjunction with DNA analyses to help clarify the taxonomy of this species and contribute towards ongoing global conservation efforts.

Straw was discovered in the right flipper where the bone had been replaced with realistic plaster reconstructions.

LiDAR scans of the blue whale skull enabling accurate measurements to be taken of it.

CHAPTER 4
A NEW POSE

The installation of the blue whale skeleton in the Whale Hall in February 1934 was a triumph and attracted huge crowds to the Museum. From mid-1934 onwards it was surrounded by four other magnificent whale specimens – a sperm whale, grey whale, North Atlantic right whale and bowhead whale. All five skeletons were mounted in a very utilitarian pose, common at the time, with the skull in line with the horizontal spine and the pectoral flippers flat against the ribcage, poses designed to show off the proportions of the whales.

Though the Chief Preparator Percy Stammwitz had spent time aboard ship in the South Atlantic and at the British whaling station on South Georgia in the 1913 to 1914 whaling season, his observations of the movement of large whales would have been very limited, so their complex behaviours could not be adequately recorded. This and the limitations of available space, once all specimens had been installed in the Whale Hall, meant that the poses did not accurately depict whales in their natural environment.

The new display of the blue whale skeleton in the voluminous Hintze Hall was intended to make effective use of the space, though not overwhelm it. A decision was made that the whale should be positioned diving down from above. Plans were drafted showing the approximate position the skeleton should occupy and, using the LiDAR scans, designers were able to produce 3D versions of Hintze Hall with the whale skeleton in position. Now it

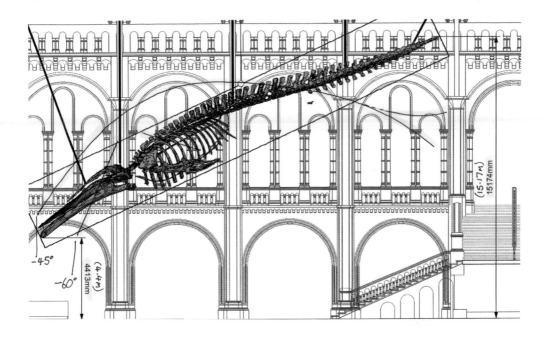

The following labels appear on the drawing:

(15·17m) 15174mm

-45°

-60° (4·4m) 4413mm

was possible to determine its exact dimensions and place it virtually within its new home. The tip of the lower jaw could not be lower than 4.4 metres (14½ feet) from the floor – low enough to create a dramatic effect for visitors entering from the main entrance doors but prevent them from being able to touch the specimen – whilst the end of the spine could be no higher than 15.17 metres (49¾ feet), which would prevent interference with overhead fire detection systems.

Richard was presented with the task of researching a new pose – one that would bring the skeleton to life, showcase the huge amount of knowledge being gathered from field observations of blue whales in their natural environment and portray how

The computer-generated drawing of Hintze Hall and the blue whale skeleton using data from 3D LiDAR scans. It shows Richard's sketch plan for the dynamic lunge-feeding pose.

remarkably streamlined blue whales are. Turning to studies of biomechanics, hydrodynamics and energetics he focused his attention on the lunge-feeding behaviour of blue whales. Growing use has been made of tagging devices containing data-loggers, which can be harmlessly attached to whales using suction cups, allowing real-time tracking of their movements. Their underwater behaviour – duration and depth of dives, angles of descent and ascent, acceleration and orientation of their bodies during feeding – can be recorded using tags fixed to the outside of the body. The tags only remain attached for a period of several hours, or no more than one or two days, after which time they float to the surface and transmit a signal that allows them to be recovered by boat. Scientific research papers listing thousands of pieces of data, and high-quality video and audio, are available online, and for three months in 2015, Richard was immersed in scientific literature, attended conferences and spoke to colleagues working with marine mammals.

While deep in research Richard was given an opportunity he couldn't turn down – the Natural History Museum had been in discussion with the BBC, which was eager to record the transformation of Hintze Hall through the science documentary television programme *Horizon*. Over the course of almost two years, the *Horizon* team recorded every stage of the removal of the *Diplodocus* cast and the installation of the blue whale. Richard outlined his ideas for presenting the whale in a lunge-feeding posture to *Horizon*, discussed the key workers in the field and how one group in particular – the Cascadia Research Collective co-founded and led by research biologist John Calambokidis – was influential in their study of whales. Since 1979, John and his colleagues have been studying the biology of marine mammals and the impact of human activity on them. Within a few weeks, a field trip had been arranged for Richard to join John and his team as they collected data from eastern North Pacific blue whales.

On a cool and misty weekday morning, Richard and a crew from the BBC headed to the harbour in Santa Barbara, California to meet John aboard two 8.5-metre- (28-foot) long, rigid inflatable boats. The plan was to head out approximately 20 nautical miles (37 kilometres) or so into the deep water channel off Santa Cruz Island. At certain times of the year, large concentrations of krill in the channel attract dozens of feeding blue whales – a perfect opportunity to observe their behaviour and movements. John and his team were planning to deploy as many data-recording tags as they possibly could onto the blue whales. The deep waters off Santa Cruz Island are where huge container ships heading to the vast port of Los Angeles come into contact with the feeding blue whales. Fatal injuries caused by ship strikes were a problem for the blue whales, and John's team had been collecting data about their movements and feeding behaviour for years, passing reports to the authorities and making recommendations for their conservation. Listening for the sound of blue whales surfacing and exhaling – or blowing – would help them locate their position, as well as the sometimes 'fishy' smell of a blue whale's blow on the wind.

Emerging from a fog bank into brilliant sunshine, less than 20 metres (66 feet) from the boat on the port side, an enormous blue whale rose to the

A scientist attaches a tag containing data-loggers to a blue whale. A suction cup holds the tag in place, causing no harm to the animal.

surface. It was unmistakable; the broad, flat, U-shaped head with its central ridge running from the tip of the upper jaw to the blowholes. The colour – a glistening blue-grey with a mottling of lighter spots – stood out against the blue water of the Pacific Ocean. The whale came to the surface and then blew a tall column of water vapour several metres into the air. Resting at the surface for a minute or so, the whale then began to cruise forward using the gentle thrust from its enormous tail flukes. It was getting ready to dive, taking deep breaths to store the oxygen it would need as it searched for food. Sure enough, the whale extended its pectoral flippers away from its body, raised its head momentarily then arched its back as it began to plunge beneath the waves. Richard watched the long, streamlined body curve through the water and finally saw the huge tail rise above the surface as the whale went into a sharp dive. Through the clear, flat, calm water left behind in the whale's wake, Richard could see how the animal moved and the cruciform shape it had when seen from above, with its flippers outstretched and its tail moving up and down. It was something he was able to observe many times over the next few days. John's team were able to anticipate the movement of a whale as it surfaced from a dive, quickly positioning the boat near to the head and leaning out from the bow with a data-tag attached to a long, flexible pole. Once the tag was in place, the boat would swiftly manoeuvre away before its presence disturbed the whale. Using this technique, they were able to successfully deploy tags onto several blue whales and gather large quantities of valuable data.

Returning to the Museum, Richard now had everything he needed to finalise his vision for the blue whale skeleton in Hintze Hall – she would be diving down towards the main entrance, lunge-feeding with mouth open wide, pectoral flippers outstretched, back arched and tail kicking upwards – mimicking the remarkable acrobatics of the blue whale. But whether a new diving pose could be achieved was something of a challenge. A more dynamic pose would be totally different from the original 1934 mount, and the new stresses placed on the skeleton had to be considered. Before committing to the new armature design and construction, data from the LiDAR scan of the whale was used to produce a 3D print in a smaller scale so that the team could articulate the model skeleton in order to refine the final position. The model produced was around 1.5 metres (5 feet) long. The Museum's team of joiners and painters created a scale replica of Hintze Hall and this was used to suspend the model skeleton across the arches to see how the specimen might look in 3D.

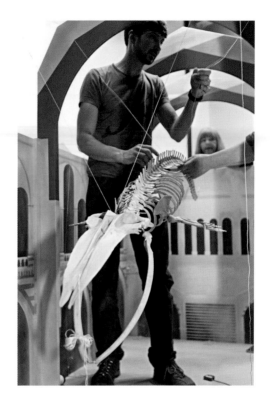

A model of the blue whale skeleton is suspended in a replica of Hintze Hall, both made to the same scale.

Three-dimensional printing, or additive manufacturing, is a process of making 3D solid objects from a digital file. The scanned information is used to form virtual slices of the object that are then fed to a 3D printer. Each layer is then 'printed' in succession and fused together during the process to create the three-dimensional object. The printing machine uses an inkjet-like printing head, which moves across a bed of powder, selectively depositing a liquid binding material to the shape of the skeleton slice. A fresh layer of powder is spread across the top of the model, and the process is repeated until the piece

is finished. When the model is complete, unbound powder is automatically removed.

A 3D printed bone is removed from the printing machine and excess unused powder is brushed from the surface.

The scale model was not the only thing that needed to be printed in 3D. A previous examination of the whale skeleton had led to the discovery that the phalanges ('finger' bones) of the right-side pectoral flipper were actually made of plaster of Paris (except for one). By mirror–imaging data from the phalanges of the left-side pectoral flipper, 3D replicas were printed to replace those made of plaster of Paris on the right. Here perhaps, was evidence of the careless loss of smaller bones during de-fleshing of the whale in 1891 that caused the Museum's Keeper of Zoology Albert Günther such anxiety.

The printed 3D phalange ('finger' bones) replacements for the right flipper.

A SPACE TO CREATE

Making a new whale armature takes up a lot of room – room not available at the Museum – so a secure facility close to London and large enough to house and build a blue whale had to be found. Eventually an aircraft hangar in Oxfordshire was located but to make it whale-friendly, and meet conservation and Research Casting International requirements, the building had to be sectioned off and fitted with basic air-conditioning to control large changes in temperature and humidity, which could damage the whale bone.

In January 2017, with the conservation work almost complete, the whale skeleton was moved out of the Museum and transported to its new temporary home in Oxfordshire. Between January and April 2017 the armature was fabricated, and regular visits were made by the team to monitor progress and carry out final conservation on parts of the skull that had previously been inaccessible.

It was obvious that various areas of the 1934 armature design were causing some structural damage, especially true for the mandible attachments and supports. A new approach was needed to ensure that the skeleton was more evenly supported across its length and that the skull and mandibles were given increased support. The challenge was to also ensure that the armature was discreet and not a distraction for visitors once the specimen was on display in Hintze Hall. An external steel cradle was hand fabricated to support the underside of the skull, providing increased support for this heaviest part of the skeleton, reducing the stress level for the bone and ensuring increased safety for Museum visitors. Only existing drilled holes in the skull and mandibles were to be used to help secure the steel cradle and bone together. The use of the 3D print, digital 3D visualisations and computer-aided design drawings enabled the teams to complete the armature design process more quickly and easily than their 1930s predecessors. The fabrication and shaping of the steel armature were carried out using hand and mechanical benders, heat and welding, allowing for a bespoke modular armature system to be produced.

Along the longer parts of the steel armature, which supported the vertebrae, joints were built in so that there was some slight flexibility to allow for any movement during the process of lifting the whale to its final position.

All areas where the bone came into contact with the steel armature were protected with a special synthetic moleskin lining to help stop abrasion to the bone. The intervertebral discs, which had previously been made from plaster and newspaper, were replaced with a more stable black conservation grade foam. The armature was painted in three colours – 'bone' colour where the armature was cradling the bone, a darker version painted onto the metal tube section which went through the neural canal of the vertebral column and a dark brown/grey colour for all armature that was not cradling the bone (which closely matched the colour of the mounts for other specimens on display in Hintze Hall).

Foam discs to enable the spacing between the vertebrae to be accurately measured.

TAKING SHAPE

Over the course of three months, the team worked alongside Research Casting International as they fitted the new armature to sections of the skeleton. The pectoral flippers were positioned based on Richard's design – outstretched from the body – increasing the width of the specimen dramatically from its 1934 pose, with each flipper angled slightly differently, as though the whale was about to execute a left-hand turn. Today's visitors to the Museum may notice the subtle differences in the position of each flipper, and the gentle rotation of some of the vertebrae in the whale's spine.

Over several days in April 2017, the precious cargo of skeleton and metal was transported back to South Kensington. The whale was delivered to the front of the Museum, straight through the front doors and directly into Hintze Hall. This required meticulous planning – special scaffolding was erected over the front steps with a lifting beam in place to move everything in safely. The biggest challenge was bringing in the enormous skull, still housed in its transportation crate. The Museum entrance was too narrow, so the front doors were removed, and the skull had to be rotated 90 degrees onto its side. With just a few centimetres to spare, the skull was pushed through the doors, wheeled into Hintze Hall and rotated back into a horizontal position.

A specialist crane truck delivered the whale mandible to the front of the Museum.

Piecing the skeleton back together around the new framework took several days. Starting with the assembly of the vertebral column, the whale began to take shape. Temporary vertical support stands were used to hold the 61 vertebrae and internal armature in the right position, before the rib armature was attached to both sides. Each of the 32 ribs was placed onto the frame and fixed into place, using bolts threaded through the existing holes. Other elements were then attached including the caudal chevrons, pelvic bones, sternum, scapulae and flippers.

A team member makes sure that the space between each vertebra is equal by the addition of a foam disc.

Once the main part of the skeleton was assembled, the skull was moved into position and the back of the skull was hoisted upwards to reflect the final angle at which it would be displayed. At this stage the skull was separate from the rest of the skeleton and held on more temporary vertical supports. The low-level assembly of the whale was complete. Some elements such as the mandibles and hyoid apparatus (the bones that the tongue and associated muscles and ligaments connect to) would not be attached until the skeleton was hoisted to a pre-planned height, so final preparations and adjustments were made to the skeleton while it was still easily accessible. The skeleton also underwent another surface clean and the bones were reassessed. The conservation team had deliberately left some smaller cracks and holes in the bone surface until this final phase – they were duly filled and painted to complement the colour of the bone. A loose section of the skull was also replaced. The phalanges for the right-side pectoral flipper, which were originally made of plaster of Paris, were replaced with resin 3D prints and some replica carpal bones were embedded into an epoxy (resin) support to complete the flipper. Both flipper supports were then painted.

Before the whale was hoisted into her final position, a small ceremony was held by the Museum team. Like the original team back in 1934, who had signed their names in pencil onto the skull, the team wanted to discreetly leave their mark on the skeleton with a 2017 date. So Lorraine Cornish, Richard Sabin, Jennifer Flippance, Arianna Bernucci and Cheryl Lynn all placed their names and date in graphite on the skull where no one would see. The next people to see both sets of signatures would be decades into the future, if a time ever came to take the skeleton down. And a small-time capsule was placed inside the skull – the contents of which only the team know.

Carrying on the tradition of marking the skeleton, the 2017 team signed the skull in a discreet place.

The whale skull is moved into place in preparation for lifting the skeleton and attaching the huge mandibles.

HEAVY LIFTING

Throughout the assembly, a specialist rigging team worked high up in Hintze Hall to fix the clamps, which would hold the cables, attached to the whale, in place. Temporary cables were then attached at ceiling level to points along the armature. The postcranial part of the skeleton was slowly lifted into place, with a rigger that pulled up each of the cables.

With the whale fully supported by the cables, the temporary vertical supports were removed from underneath the skeleton and the height was adjusted so the skull could be attached. It was difficult to lift the whale without substantial lateral movement causing a slight shuddering and shaking. The temporary supports from underneath the skull were removed and the skeleton was hoisted up a few centimetres further. A temporary sling and chain support was added into the centre of the skeleton along the vertebral column to add stability and support for the final lifting phase. The lifting method was adapted to ensure even greater control and very slowly, 25 millimetres (1 inch) at a time, the skeleton was hoisted upwards to where the mandibles could be safely fixed at the agreed angle, showing the whale in its final feeding position with its jaws open. The hyoid apparatus was then attached. This was the first time that there had been enough space underneath the skull to manoeuvre such a fragile part into place. The skeleton was then hoisted to its final resting place. Lasers were used to measure the height of the skeleton from the ground during this lifting process so that the correct height could be achieved.

Finally, on the 8 May 2017, the blue whale skeleton was safely installed. Eighteen permanent cables were then attached to replace the temporary ones consisting of 10 primary and four

smaller cables, plus a further four cables to the flippers and mandibles to add the support required to keep the skeleton safely displayed. During the subsequent two months the Hintze Hall Wonder Bays and First Floor balconies were filled with specimens to complete the transformation of the hall.

In late June 2017 the conservation team inspected the whale skeleton to check for any movement or damage during the first few weeks of suspension. This involved the use of scaffolding and mobile platforms. Everything was found to be in a satisfactory condition. A final clean took place and the skeleton was ready.

Final preparations are made before the blue whale skeleton is hoisted into Hintze Hall's ceiling by a specialist rigging team.

CHAPTER 5

THE SCIENCE OF BLUE WHALES

The purchase of the Wexford blue whale skeleton by the Natural History Museum in 1891 represented a significant addition to its Cetacea research collection. Ensuring that the whale's baleen was also purchased has provided today's scientists with important material to study. It is estimated that commercial whaling had reduced numbers of North Atlantic blue whales to less than 30 per cent of their pre-whaling population by the time coordinated field studies were undertaken in the mid-twentieth century.

Natural history collections with temporal depth and spatial breadth represent an invaluable resource and provide an opportunity to examine changes to organisms and their ecosystems, whether these are driven by natural environmental processes or the impact of human activity. In the late twentieth century, science turned to museum collections to extend the datasets compiled from modern collecting and direct field observations. An overview was needed to help understand issues such as the effects of global climate change, long-term use of pesticides and other harmful pollutants, like human-generated noise in our oceans. Baseline data were required to help give scientists an understanding of how things were from a time before the effects of human population expansion were felt

across the globe. Museum collections became increasingly important for the study of evolution, biodiversity and population genetics, as valuable DNA was found to be preserved in the tissues of specimens collected centuries ago.

Understanding the genetic make-up of organisms living at a time before populations were decimated by human or natural processes, has helped scientists to calculate the rates and effects of biodiversity loss. In addition, it became clear that many museum specimens contained important traces of elements – known as stable isotopes – which could be used to help understand the migratory routes, diets and positions within food chains of organisms. The development of new analytical techniques has created a renaissance for museum collections.

The individual 3D scanning of each bone of the blue whale skeleton has allowed a digital version of the specimen to be created. From a specimen conservation perspective, this has provided a hugely important record of the skeleton's condition. From the perspective of being able to study the structure and function of the entire skeleton, this is unparalleled anywhere else in the world and represents a valuable scientific resource. For example, the biomechanics of blue whale feeding are poorly

A 3D digital model of Hope, created by surface scanning each individual bone.

understood. When a blue whale opens its mouth and engulfs a concentration of krill, the pleated throat pouch of the animal expands and the resulting mass of prey and seawater can weigh as much as the whale itself. The blue whale uses its tongue to push water out through its plates of baleen, effectively filtering the krill and allowing it to swallow its food. The bones of the lower jaw cope with incredible stresses placed upon them by the engulfment. This is the biggest single feeding action on the planet by the largest animal ever known to have lived, and the digital data created by the scanning of the whale's skeleton are allowing this process to be studied in detail.

Data collected from the skeleton will be used to address questions about blue whale movement and speed, whilst other data are helping researchers study the evolution of cetacean skulls and hearing in large whale species. As more scans are completed of the skulls of blue whales from around the world, a digital dataset with more statistical significance about physical and geographical diversity is being created. This can be examined to make comparisons between living whales and the fossils of extinct cetacean species.

A lunge-feeding blue whale with a distended throat pouch full of krill.

An individual krill. Krill, small shrimp-like crustaceans, are the primary food source of blue whales.

In further research, scientists have been using a technique, known as stable isotope analysis, to investigate Hope's final movements. Because carbon is naturally found in the environment in two different forms or isotopes, one heavy and one light, and because different parts of the world have distinctive ratios of these isotopes, scientists can look at these ratios in living tissues and use them to infer where in the world an organism was when it built those tissues.

In 2017, samples were taken from the more than 400 plates of baleen collected from the Wexford blue whale for stable isotope analysis. Baleen is made of keratin, an inert protein also found in human hair and fingernails, which grows throughout the whale's life but wears away at the ends over time. Hope's baleen records her final seven years of life and scientists were able to reconstruct her likely movement patterns by comparing the stable carbon isotopes in her baleen to values in the North Atlantic. Current modern research suggests that North Atlantic blue whales migrate between their feeding sites in Greenland and Iceland and their breeding sites in the Azores. The results from Hope's baleen

Sequential arrangement of Hope's baleen plates. The bristled fringes of the plates act as a highly effective filter to help catch krill.

suggest she spent two years in warm waters around Mauritania/ Cape Verde or the Azores, followed by three years migrating north in the summer to feed on the abundant krill at ocean upwelling sites north of Iceland and Norway, then south in the winter to avoid the frozen polar seas. In her final year, Hope migrated back down to warm equatorial waters and remained there for almost a year. We can't be sure, but she may have had a calf and weaned it during this time, before moving north again and stranding in March 1891. So perhaps her descendants are still swimming in the North Atlantic today.

It is hoped that information derived from the baleen samples will add further detail to data gathered from satellite tracking and other observations of modern blue whale movements, and that it will help provide an insight into the feeding strategies of fossil whale species.

Through its actions, the research generated by the Museum will be of value to the broader understanding of blue whales and aid in their conservation in the wild. The digitisation of the skeleton has raised the profile of the Museum's research collection, and online digital content has been created and is available on its website, helping to extend access to its collections to people around the world.

HOPE FOR THE FUTURE

On the 25 March 2017 on the 126th anniversary of the blue whale's death, Richard Sabin stood on the spot where her body had lain all those years before, on the beautiful coast of Wexford in Ireland. The whale had been named Hope by the Natural History Museum, as a symbol of humanity's power to shape a sustainable future. Richard was in Ireland to investigate Hope's

human story and add depth to her interpretation. He met the descendants of Ned Wickham, the man who first saw Hope, and learned how important the whale is to the history of Wexford. He was able to learn more about the events surrounding Hope's appearance in Irish waters, her subsequent death and the involvement of local people in preparing her bones for transportation to London. Most importantly, he felt the sense of connection that the people of Wexford still had to Hope, and their pride in knowing that she was to become the central specimen at the heart of the Natural History Museum in London.

The unveiling of Hope in Hintze Hall in July 2017 was an international media event. On the same day as her launch, the BBC broadcast the *Horizon* programme, *Dippy and the Whale*, which had followed the progress of the transformation and work of Museum staff for more than two years. Critically acclaimed as

Richard Sabin standing on the beach at The Raven, on the north side of Wexford Harbour, Ireland, 25 March 2017.

an awe-inspiring new icon of the Museum, her diving, lunge-feeding form set against the stunning backdrop of Alfred Waterhouse's architecture, took people's breath away. Sir Michael Dixon, Director of the Museum said: 'This is a landmark moment for the Museum and for the millions of people from all over the world who visit us. The transformation of Hintze Hall represents a new era for us as a natural history museum for the future. Putting our blue whale, Hope, at the centre of the Museum, between living species on the West and extinct species on the East, is a powerful reminder of the fragility of life and the responsibility we have towards our planet. We are living at a critical point in the history of the Earth. This generation's decisions will have an unprecedented impact on the world we live in. It is within the grasp of humanity

Museum Patron, Her Royal Highness, The Duchess of Cambridge with Museum Director Sir Michael Dixon meet Lorraine and Richard at the formal unveiling of Hope in July 2017.

to shape a future that is sustainable, and now more than ever we want our galleries and exhibitions to inspire a love of the natural world, and our scientific expertise to inform solutions to the big, global challenges we face.'

In 1966, the International Whaling Commission banned the commercial hunting of blue whales, a ban which is still in place in 2018, and is respected by all nations. International cooperation ensured that the mass slaughter of the species came to an end. It was the first time that our human species took a decision to prevent another species from sliding into extinction. Hope is an emblem of the damage we can cause through our irresponsibility and our greed, and the optimism to be drawn from our power to effect positive change to our world. Blue whales had been reduced in numbers from around 350,000 worldwide at the beginning of the twentieth century, to perhaps just a few thousand by 1966. Data suggest that in some areas numbers are now increasing, which is encouraging, but this does not mean that we can become complacent. Now, more than ever, our activities can be shown to have a direct effect on our planet and for the sake of future generations of people and for all life on Earth, we must act responsibly and work together across all nations.

Hope on display in Hintze Hall in her dynamic diving pose reflecting the way blue whales feed.

SUGGESTED READING

Bernucci, A., Cornish, L. and Lynn, C. (2017). A modern approach to dismantling and redisplaying a historic blue whale skeleton. ICOM-CC-publications online, Copenhagen.

Goldbogen, J. A., Calambokidis, J., Oleson, E., Potvin, J., Pyenson, N. D., Schorr, G. and Shadwick, R. E. (2011). Mechanics, hydrodynamics and energetics of blue whale lunge feeding: efficiency dependence on krill density. *Journal of Experimental Biology*, 214: 131–146.

Goldbogen, J. A., Calambokidis, J., Friedlaender, A. S., Francis, J., DeRuiter, S. L., Stimpert, A. K., Falcone, E. and Southall, B. L. (2013). Underwater acrobatics by the world's largest predator: 360° rolling manoeuvres by lunge-feeding blue whales. *Biology Letters*.

Hammond, P., Heinrich, S., Hooker, S. and Tyack, P. (2017). *Whales – their Past, Present and Future*. Natural History Museum, London.

Stearn, W.T. (1981). *The Natural History Museum at South Kensington*. Natural History Museum, London.

ACKNOWLEDGEMENTS

Special thanks to all the various teams across the Museum who worked tirelessly to enable Hope to move to her new home in Hintze Hall, especially: Arianna Bernucci, Cheryl Lynn and the rest of the conservation team; Jennifer Flippance who project managed the move; Natalie Cooper, Researcher, Department of Life Sciences; Andrea Hart, Library Special Collections Manager; Bucy McDonald, Senior Film Producer and Callum Mair, Digital Media Producer, Film Unit. Thanks also to: Liz Shiel, Mary Costello and other descendants of Ned Wickham; Alison Williams, descendant of William Armstrong; Charles Gerrard, Bari and Robert Logan (for keeping the whale's tail-bone safe); Annie Mackinder, Producer/Director, BBC (*Horizon*); Gráinne Doran, Archivist, Wexford County Archive, Ireland; Captain Phil Murphy, County Wexford Harbour Master, Ireland; Nigel Monahan, Keeper of Natural History, The National Museum of Ireland, Dublin; John Calambokidis, Research Biologist and co-founder of the Cascadia Research Collective, Olympia, Washington, USA; Clive Trueman, Associate Professor in Marine Ecology, National Oceanography Centre, Southampton, UK; the team at Research Casting International, Canada and Ron and Margaret Sabin (for giving Richard the money to go to the Museum on a school trip from Birmingham when he was 10 years old).

PICTURE CREDITS